THE
PRINCE OF WALES' BOOK

To Alice
with love from

Nancy & George

———

April 5th
1921,

COPYRIGHT CANADA 1919
PRINGLE & BOOTH TORONTO

Edward P.

THE
PRINCE of WALES'
BOOK

A PICTORIAL RECORD OF THE
VOYAGES OF H.M.S. "RENOWN"
1919—1920

PUBLISHED FOR ST. DUNSTAN'S

BY

HODDER & STOUGHTON, LTD

LONDON   NEW YORK   TORONTO

ENGRAVED AND
PRINTED IN PHOTOGRAVURE
IN GREAT BRITAIN
BY
THE SUN ENGRAVING
COMPANY, LTD.
LONDON & WATFORD

I hope that all who can will buy this book of photographs and will thus help me to secure the largest possible assistance for our sailors and soldiers who were blinded in the War.

Edward P.

Introduction

I AM publishing this book of photographs for the benefit of St. Dunstan's, the hostel for blinded sailors and soldiers in Regent's Park. The hostel, and all the splendid care which it has given to sightless men, are due in the first instance to Sir Arthur Pearson, with whom a large staff has worked with untiring devotion since 1915. The house and grounds in which the work of St. Dunstan's has been done it owes to the generosity of an American citizen, Mr. Otto Kahn.

Twelve hundred men have passed through St. Dunstan's during the last five years. Five hundred are there now or are about to go there very soon. These include 88 Canadians, 81 Australians, 23 New Zealanders, and 13 South Africans. St. Dunstan's has therefore served the Dominions no less than the Old Country, and it has received the most splendid tributes from all those whom it has trained.

I want to call special attention to the word "trained." St. Dunstan's is not a hospital, it is a university where men are taught to live again and to enjoy their life despite the loss of sight. Not only does it set them up in trades with wonderful success, but it watches and assists them afterwards with materials, with information, and with skilled advice. In this way its utility will continue long after the last of its students has gone out with new hope into the world; and their welfare will depend in large measure upon its ability to keep personal touch with them and to supply their special needs.

With this object I have commandeered a great deal of work and help, which have been given for sheer sympathy with the cause. I want therefore to express my gratitude to Messrs. Hodder and Stoughton for undertaking the publication of the book; to Lord Riddell and the News-paper Proprietors' Association, to the Central News, to Sir George McLaren Brown, European General Manager of the Canadian Pacific Railway, to Messrs. Pringle & Booth of Toronto, to Messrs. Raines and Co., to Messrs. Underwood and Underwood of New York, and to the Topical Press Agency, for valuable assistance in connexion with the photographs; and also to many unknown photo-graphers, whose snapshots, presented to me during the two tours, I have taken the liberty to use. I am sure the latter will be glad to have helped me in making what I hope will be great success of this book.

EDWARD P.

THE
CANADIAN TOUR

THE Prince of Wales left Portsmouth for Canada in H.M.S. *Renown* on August 5th, 1919. He arrived at Portsmouth again on December 1st. During that period of four months he had visited Newfoundland, every province of the Dominion of Canada from Nova Scotia to British Columbia, and had also made a short stay of about a fortnight in the United States. The greater part of this stay was devoted to Washington and New York. A short interval between the two was spent in comparative seclusion at White Sulphur Springs, Western Virginia, where he lived at the well-known hotel and played golf.

The photographs which follow illustrate practically every phase of the tour. Many have been contributed by private individuals, and have never been published before. Others are the work of professional photographers, and have appeared from time to time in newspapers and magazines. In selecting them for this book the more formal, such as photographs of official groups, have as a rule been omitted, and a general preference has been given to less official pictures and to snapshots.

There is no need to preface such a collection with a detailed diary of the Prince of Wales's movements. A very brief outline will suffice to explain the order in which the photographs are arranged.

H.M.S. *Renown*, with the Prince of Wales on board,

arrived at Conception Bay, Newfoundland, on August 11. After a quiet day, spent mainly in a good walk ashore, the Prince and his Staff trans-shipped to the escorting light cruiser, H.M.S. *Dragon*, which entered the harbour of the capital, St. John's, early next morning, while the *Renown* went on to Halifax. From Newfoundland the *Dragon* conveyed the Prince to St. John, the capital of New Brunswick, where he made his first landing on Canadian soil on August 15th. The Governor-General, the Duke of Devonshire, and the Prime Minister of the Dominion, Sir Robert Borden, welcomed the Prince to Canada in St. John, where a short pageant was arranged close by the landing-stage to represent the greeting of all the provinces of the Dominion. Most unfortunately the weather was wet, but the pageant was very prettily carried through amidst great enthusiasm, and no amount of rain could have damped the ardour of the crowds gathered to receive him throughout the city. From St. John the *Dragon* bore him to Halifax, the capital of Nova Scotia, where he returned to the *Renown*. From Halifax the route lay through the Gut of Canso to Charlottetown, the capital of Prince Edward Island, and thence up the St. Lawrence River to Quebec. In spite of a fog in the St. Lawrence not many miles below Quebec, which made the last stage of the voyage a little hazardous, the *Renown* anchored off the Citadel of Quebec, under the Heights of Abraham, punctually to programme time on August 21st.

Up to this point the Prince of Wales had lived entirely in the *Renown* and the *Dragon*, except for one night ashore at Government House, St. John's, Newfoundland. Both ships remained in the stream at Quebec during his residence there, and few will forget the beauty of the evening when town and ships were picked out in brilliant lines of light for the Governor-General's Ball in the old rooms of the Citadel, standing out upon the historic bluff which looks across the broad reach of the St. Lawrence to the island below and the shore beyond. After the Prince of Wales's departure from Quebec the crews of both ships were hospitably entertained in several of the nearer cities of Canada, and both then went upon their occasions elsewhere. The *Renown* paid a visit to the West Indies and to South America, returning to pick up the Prince of Wales in November at New York.

The Prince of Wales left Quebec in the great train which had been prepared with every care to carry him across the Dominion and back again. He himself lived in the rearmost car. This consisted of three sleeping cabins, occupied by himself and two members of his Staff; a small dining-room, in which he and the whole Staff (ten in all) took their meals; a sitting-room, furnished with easy chairs and a gramophone, which did yeoman service throughout the tour; and an observation platform at the very rear from which he could always easily be seen as the train steamed away. This car was the private property of Lord Shaughnessy, who had very kindly put it at the Prince's disposal. Its colouring of light satinwood and blue will long remain in the memories of those who made the tour. The remainder of the Staff and suite were accommodated in adjoining cars. The other cars of the long train—which never totalled less than twelve cars— were occupied by a powerful staff of railway and other representatives deputed to accompany the tour by the Dominion Government, the Canadian Pacific Railway, the Provincial Governments, and the British and Canadian Press.

From Quebec the route lay to Toronto, where a crowd of many thousands could congregate in the Exhibition Grounds by the lake-side. The scene which greeted the

Prince's first arrival there was indescribable. It was his first experience of crowds on that tremendous scale, and his first meeting with a very large body of returned soldiers. The enthusiasm culminated on the last afternoon, when he drove for nearly three hours through densely packed and wildly cheering multitudes along all Toronto's principal streets. The same scenes were afterwards repeated in all the great cities of Canada.

From Toronto the Prince of Wales went to Ottawa, where he was for several days the guest of the Governor-General at Rideau Hall, and laid the foundation stone of the Victory Tower, which is to form part of the new buildings of the Dominion Parliament. On his way west from Ottawa he spent a memorable three hours in Montreal, which welcomed him with the same intense enthusiasm as Toronto, and then continued his steady progress to the Prairie Provinces, turning aside for three days' fishing en route on the Nipigon River. He reached Winnipeg, the capital of Manitoba, on September 9th, and travelled thence to Saskatoon, the second city of Saskatchewan and the seat of the Provincial University. Edmonton, the capital of Alberta, came next, and after it Calgary, the famous railway centre at the foot of the great barrier of the Rocky Mountains. After leaving Calgary the Prince paid a short visit to the Bar-U Ranch, and then spent four or five days amid the splendours of that magnificent range at Banff, Lake Louise, and Emerald Lake, passing thence across the Selkirks by Revelstoke and reaching Vancouver on September 22nd.

The Western end of the tour was reached at Victoria, the beautiful capital of British Columbia, which lies on Vancouver Island across a lovely stretch of blue water studded with dark green islands and overlooked by the mountains of the Olympic Range.

THE CANADIAN TOUR

Two days of official ceremonies at Victoria were followed by three or four devoted to recreation and a short tour in the interior of Vancouver Island ; and on September 28th the Prince turned East again. The Selkirks and Rocky Mountains were crossed this time by the more southern route, which took the Prince through the beauties of the Okanagan Valley, the Arrowhead Lakes, and the Kootenay District, and thence by Crow's Nest's Pass down upon Medicine Hat. From that busy centre, with its strange Indian name and its amazing supply of natural gas, the way led by Moose Jaw to Regina, the capital of Saskatchewan. Between Regina and Winnipeg the Prince enjoyed three days' good duck-shooting amid intense cold, and then resumed his journey eastward round the head of the Great Lakes to the rich agricultural and fruit-growing country of South-West Ontario and Niagara Falls. He reached Montreal for the final week of his official programme on October 27th. The wonderful scenes at Toronto at the outset of his journey West were renewed at Montreal on his return. Those two great cities seem to frame the continuous triumph of his progress across the Dominion and back again.

After leaving Montreal the Prince paid a short and unofficial return visit to Toronto, and went thence to Ottawa for a few days' quiet before his official visit to the President of the United States at Washington. He saw the last of his Canadian train there, for the American Government sent up its own train to fetch him from Ottawa on November 10th.

He arrived at Washington next morning, and remained there as the guest of the United States Government till November 14th, when he went South for his short holiday at White Sulphur Springs. On November 18th he entered New York, leaving his train at Jersey City and crossing the Hudson to make his official landing at the Battery, where New York receives all its honoured visitors from oversea. The stay in New York, which lasted four days, was one long riot of public engagements and popular enthusiasm. Nothing could have exceeded the kindness and hospitality of its people to their British guest. On November 22nd the Prince of Wales went down the Hudson in the *Renown*, escorted by the U.S.S. *Delaware* and a detachment of United States ships, and steamed up to Halifax to take his final leave of the Government and people of Canada. The last farewells were spoken at a small dinner on shore and a final luncheon next day on board the *Renown*. The ship steamed out of Halifax harbour just before sunset on November 25th, and the great tour was over.

There is no occasion here to describe the more official side of the tour, with its banquets, its speeches and addresses, and the more or less formal ceremonies by which these are accompanied everywhere. It may, however, assist the story told by the photographs to pick out four striking features of the visit which distinguish it from other progresses of the same kind.

The first and most striking of these was an outcome of the great war. Many of the returned soldiers had known the Prince of Wales at the front in France, Flanders, and Germany. When he reached Canada they flocked in their thousands to greet him, not only at every place where he stopped, but at many places through which his train had to pass without stopping at all. He made it his custom, wherever the numbers permitted, to shake hands with every man and also, wherever possible, to shake hands with and speak to the relatives of the fallen. It is difficult to say which of the two kinds of tribute paid by the soldiers was the most touching—the massive gatherings in great cities like Toronto, Montreal, and Winnipeg, where thousands of men were on parade, or the little parties waiting at wayside stations, often in the middle of the night, many of them having come across rough country or prairie by journeys of many hours by horse or buggy or car. Again and again the train was stopped for two or three minutes at the Prince's own request, while he stepped off to have a few words with the waiting people and shake their hands.

Hardly less striking in their way were the gatherings of school-children, which were a feature of his reception everywhere. As with the soldiers, these gatherings varied from many hundreds to little parties collected from the prairie at any wayside station through which the train passed. Every child, as a rule, had a little Union Jack to wave, and most of the schools sang gallantly through "O Canada" and "God Bless the Prince of Wales." The Prince himself almost invariably said a few words to the children, whose appreciation was always much enhanced by the extra whole holiday which he procured for them.

Not less memorable, and at times completely overwhelming in their enthusiasm, were the throngs which gathered to cheer him as he drove through the streets. In many places the desire to get near to him was so strong that his car would be densely thronged for miles, while girls clambered on the steps to throw him flowers, to touch him, or to beg for an autograph. There was never a less formal type of procession than these drives which he made through all parts of the great cities visited during the tour.

At Toronto on August 25th the Prince of Wales made a further innovation by holding a popular reception in the City Hall, at which he shook hands with all who wished to do so and were able to reach the hall in time. After he had shaken hands for more than two hours, and long before all the waiting crowds had succeeded in filing past him, his programme obliged him to stop, and he could only go out upon a balcony and express his great regret at not having time to shake hands with the many hundreds still waiting below. Popular receptions of this kind were afterwards held in all the chief cities of the Dominion, but the Prince later abandoned the attempt to shake hands in order that more people might be able to pass him at close quarters in the available time.

No record of the Canadian tour, however sketchy, would be adequate without reference to one other feature which figures in the photographs. The Indian tribes were as eager as any to show their loyalty and to greet him with the traditional ceremonies of their race. At Banff and elsewhere he was made a chieftain and christened with a new Indian name. On most of these occasions he was presented with an Indian warrior's trappings, and wore them while the Indian ceremony was being carried out. One of the photographs in this collection depicts him in the full dress of a Red Indian chief.

In a few touching words of farewell, spoken at Halifax on the Prince's last night in the Dominion, Sir Robert Borden quoted the call to Prince Charlie in the old Royalist song :—

"Better lo'ed ye canna be ;
Will ye no come back again ?"

And all Canadians knew that as they loved the Prince, so and no less the Prince himself loved Canada and them.

The
Canadian
Tour

AS A NAVAL OFFICER

AS AN INDIAN CHIEF

PORTSMOUTH

DEPARTURE FOR CANADA,
AUGUST 5th, 1919

THE ROYAL FAMILY
WITH THE OFFICERS
ON BOARD THE " RENOWN "

NEWFOUNDLAND

IN FRONT OF COLONIAL BUILDING, ST. JOHNS

RECEIVES AN ADDRESS AT ST. JOHNS

CANADA

LANDING IN CANADA

THE PAGEANT OF PROVINCES, NEW BRUNSWICK

INSPECTING VETERANS, HALIFAX

CANADA

PLACES A WREATH
ON
CHAMPLAIN MONUMENT,
QUEBEC

SIGNS
THE VISITORS'
BOOK

DECORATING AGED VETERAN

IN BATTLEFIELD PARK, QUEBEC

SALUTE FROM CITADEL, QUEBEC

CANADA

DECORATING
VETERANS
OF THE
GREAT WAR

ON
THE
PLAINS
OF ABRAHAM

AT WOLFE'S MONUMENT, QUEBEC

CANADA

ARRIVING AT ST. ANNE DE BEAUPRE

IN THE STREETS OF ST. ANNE

CANADA

DECORATING SOLDIERS AT TORONTO

" GOD SAVE THE KING "

CANADA

AT TORONTO EXHIBITION

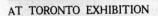

A TORONTO CROWD

CANADA

CHILDREN
CLIMB LAMP-POSTS
TO SEE
THE PRINCE

OUTSIDE
PARLIAMENT
BUILDINGS,
OTTAWA

ALL CLASSES WELCOME THE PRINCE

CANADA

THREE CHEERS
FOR THE KING

AT THE LAYING OF THE CORNER-STONE, PARLIAMENT BUILDINGS, OTTAWA

SIR ROBERT BORDEN, PREMIER OF CANADA

CANADA

AT SAULT STE MARIE

AT SUDBURY

CANADA

BY THE SOO CANAL

"GOOD-BYE"

SPEAKING AT SAULT STE MARIE

WITH THE GUIDES ON THE NIPIGON RIVER

CANADA

AT VIRGIN FALLS

PASSING DOWN THE NIPIGON

D

CANADA

WITH THE
INDIAN
GUIDES

ON THE WAY
TO THE TRAIN

ARRIVING AT CAMERON FALLS

CANADA

WITH GENERAL
SIR H. BURSTALL

IN CAMP

LEAVING NIPIGON

CANADA

ON THE UNIVERSITY CAMPUS, WINNIPEG

PUBLIC RECEPTION AT WINNIPEG

WITH THE LIEUT: GOVERNOR OF MANITOBA

CANADA

AT THE RECEPTION, WINNIPEG

FATHER DANDURAND (AGED 101) COMES TO SEE THE
PRINCE AT THE POPULAR RECEPTION

CANADA

WITH THE MAYOR OF SASKATOON

GREATLY TO THE DELIGHT OF THE COWBOYS
H.R.H. LED THEM UP THE COURSE

ROPING STEERS
AT THE STAMPEDE

CANADA

ON A COW-PONY
AT STAMPEDE

TALKING WITH
A COW-GIRL

AT THE SASKATOON STAMPEDE

CANADA

AT SASKATOON

WITH THE LIEUT: GOVERNOR OF ALBERTA

CANADA

AT THE BASE-BALL MATCH, EDMONTON

CHEERING THE ROYAL PITCHER

CANADA

AUTOGRAPHS
THE BALL HE TOSSED
IN THE GAME BETWEEN
" EDMONTON VETS " AND
" CALGARY HUSTLERS "

RECEIVING HONORARY LL.D. AT EDMONTON UNIVERSITY

CANADA

AN IMPROMPTU SPEECH
AT HIGH RIVER STATION

WITH GEORGE LANE AT BAR U RANCH

CANADA

CUTTING OUT
CATTLE

THE CATTLE ROUND-UP, BAR U

CANADA

CHIEF
MORNING STAR

PRESENTING AN INDIAN COSTUME TO THE PRINCE AS
CHIEF MORNING STAR OF THE STONY INDIAN TRIBE

CANADA

INSPECTION OF THE
GUARD OF HONOUR,
VANCOUVER

LAYING
CORNER-STONE,
VANCOUVER

ON BOARD THE STEAMER, VANCOUVER—VICTORIA

CANADA

OUTSIDE PARLIAMENT BUILDINGS, VICTORIA

VICTORIA'S PATH OF ROSES

CANADA

PRESENTATION OF MEDALS, PARLIAMENT BUILDINGS, VICTORIA

A CHAT WITH INDIANS AT GOVERNMENT HOUSE, VICTORIA

CANADA

CHEERING HIS ROYAL HIGHNESS AT DUNCAN, B.C

AT LADYSMITH, B.C.

E

CANADA

SHAKES HANDS WITH THE WORKERS IN YARROW'S SHIPYARD, ESQUIMALT

VISITS RETURNED SOLDIERS' SETTLEMENT AND IS INITIATED INTO
THE METHOD OF CLEARING THE CUT-OVER LANDS, VANCOUVER ISLAND

CANADA

LEAVING CITY HALL—NANAIMO

LEAVING SUMMERLAND

CANADA

1. INSPECTS THE VETERANS

2. RECEIVES AN ADDRESS OF
   WELCOME AT MAPLE CREEK

3. WAVES AN ACKNOWLEDGMENT
   OF CHEERS

4. MEETS A CITY OFFICIAL

CANADA

TALKS TO MEMBERS
OF THE BAND

AT MOOSE JAW

COMPLIMENTING CITY GARDENER AT MOOSE JAW

CANADA

AT MEDICINE HAT

INSPECTING R.N.W.M.P. AT THEIR HEADQUARTERS, REGINA

CANADA

DECORATING POLICE OFFICER WITH KING'S POLICE MEDAL

CANADA

IN THE MARSHES, QU'APPELLE LAKES, SASKATCHEWAN

CANADA

PORTAGE-LA-PRAIRIE

CANADA

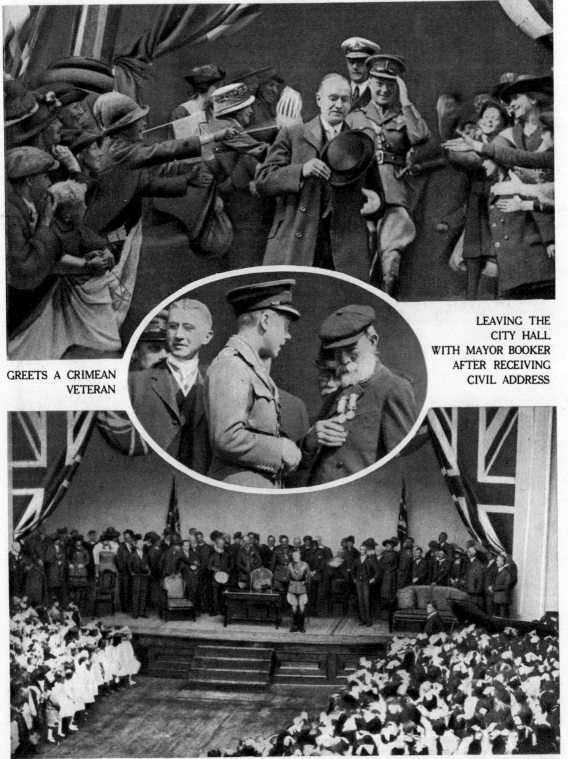

GREETS A CRIMEAN
VETERAN

LEAVING THE
CITY HALL
WITH MAYOR BOOKER
AFTER RECEIVING
CIVIL ADDRESS

OPENING NEW MEMORIAL HALL, HAMILTON

CANADA

AT HAMILTON

AT THE ROYAL MILITARY COLLEGE, KINGSTON

CANADA

AT NIAGARA FALLS, ONT.

CANADA

WAR
VETERANS
AT
CHATHAM,
ONTARIO

CANADA

WITH THE GIRL STUDENTS OF THE ONTARIO AGRICULTURAL COLLEGE, GUELPH

CANADA

ON THE WAY BACK TO OTTAWA

CANADA

AT THE CARTIER MONUMENT, MONTREAL

INSPECTION OF ALLIED TROOPS IN LAFONTAINE PARK, MONTREAL

F

WITH THE ENGINE DRIVER

RIGHT AWAY!

CANADA

AT THE THROTTLE OF No. 2231

BIDDING FAREWELL TO THE TRAIN CREW

TALKING WITH HARRY FLOOD, ENGINEER OF C.P.R. ENGINE No. 2231,
WHICH H.R.H. DROVE FROM FLAVELLE TO TRENTON, ONTARIO

CANADA

DIXIE GOLF LINKS
NEAR MONTREAL

ON THE LINKS

EXERCISE ON BOARD H.M.S. " DRAGON "

CANADA

WATCHING
FIRING FROM
SPOTTING TOP OF
H.M.S. "RENOWN"

H.R.H. AND CAPTAIN TAYLOR

ON BOARD H.M.S. "RENOWN"

THE UNITED STATES

INTERVIEWED BY THE PRESS IMMEDIATELY ON ARRIVAL

BISHOP BURCH PRESENTS A BIBLE TO THE PRINCE

PHOTOS BY UNDERWOOD & UNDERWOOD, N.Y

ARRIVAL AT UNION STATION, WASHINGTON

AT THE PEACE CROSS OF WASHINGTON CATHEDRAL

PHOTOS BY UNDERWOOD & UNDERWOOD, N.Y.

THE UNITED STATES

WITH VICE-PRESIDENT MARSHALL, AT MOUNT VERNON

LEAVING CHURCH AT WHITE SULPHUR SPRINGS, W. VIRGINIA

GOLFING AT WHITE SULPHUR SPRINGS

THE UNITED STATES

ON THE GOLF LINKS, WHITE SULPHUR SPRINGS

INSPECTS GUARD OF HONOUR ON ARRIVAL AT NEW YORK

AT THE BATTERY, NEW YORK

PHOTOS BY UNDERWOOD & UNDERWOOD, N.Y

THE UNITED STATES

ARRIVAL IN NEW YORK

ON THE STEPS OF THE CITY HALL, NEW YORK

THE UNITED STATES

REVIEWS BOY SCOUTS AT COLUMBIA YACHT CLUB

LEAVING GRANT'S TOMB

PLACES A WREATH ON JOAN OF ARC'S STATUE

VISITS WEST POINT

PHOTOS BY UNDERWOOD & UNDERWOOD, N.Y

THE UNITED STATES

REVIEWS WEST POINT CADETS

VISIT TO PIPING ROCK

PHOTOS BY UNDERWOOD & UNDERWOOD, N.Y

A WREATH ON MR. ROOSEVELT'S GRAVE

THE RECEPTION AT SEVENTH REGIMENT ARMORY, NEW YORK

THE UNITED STATES

PLANTING MEMORIAL TREES IN CENTRAL PARK, NEW YORK

AT WALTER REED HOSPITAL

ENGLAND

WITH HIS MARINE ORDERLIES

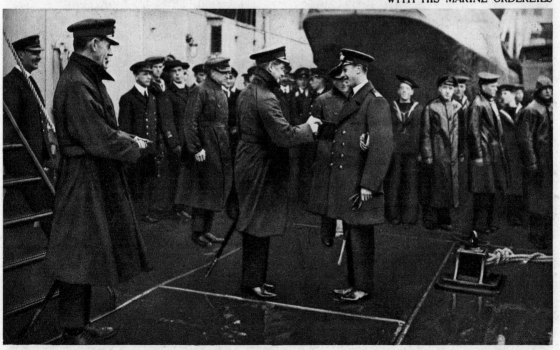

HOME AGAIN

ENGLAND

LANDING AT PORTSMOUTH, DECEMBER 1st, 1919

ARRIVING AT VICTORIA STATION, LONDON, DECEMBER 1st, 1919

THE
AUSTRALASIAN
TOUR

THE Prince of Wales's second tour extended over a period of just under seven months. He left Portsmouth, once again on board H.M.S. *Renown*, on March 16th, 1920, and returned there on October 11th.

The second tour had been much more varied in character than the first; for, in addition to the two self-governing Dominions of Australia and New Zealand, it included the British West Indian Colonies and some British Colonies in the Pacific. The Prince was also for a short period again on United States territory in the Panama Canal Zone, at San Diego, the southernmost port of California, and at Honolulu, the capital of the Hawaiian Islands.

At all three points the kindness, forethought, and hospitality of the United States authorities, and the welcome given him by the population as a whole, made the short time which he spent with them extremely agreeable. The Prince was also on foreign territory during a short visit to the city of Panama, where he was entertained most cordially by the President and Government of the Republic and for a few hours on the return journey at Acapulco, in Mexico. With those exceptions, he was at sea or on British territory throughout the whole tour.

G

The Prince's first stopping place was the ancient and loyal Colony of Barbados. He landed there on March 26th, and after the usual ceremonies in the capital went for a long drive in the country to see how the planting industries were conducted, and how the working population lived. The negro subjects of the King—the first whom the Prince had seen—showed unbounded enthusiasm everywhere. At one point where his motor stopped for a minute or two an old negro lady crept up to look at him, and then spun round in an ecstatic dance, clapping her hands and crying: "Tank de Lord, mine eyes hab seen 'im!" Her delight was typical of her people's feeling everywhere.

From Barbados the route lay across the Caribbean Sea, just north of Nombre Dios Bay, where Drake was buried at sea, to the Atlantic terminus of the Panama Canal at Cristobal. The *Renown* entered the canal early on March 30th, and emerged into the Pacific the same evening. Owing to a recent landslide in the narrowest part of the canal, the Gaillard Cut, there was very little room to spare for a ship of her length, and it was a fine piece of seamanship on the part of the canal authorities to pass her through. The scenery of the canal was very beautiful. It is surrounded by hills densely covered with tropical forest, and almost perpetually wreathed in shifting mists. The lower land by the canal itself gives it a graceful frame of palms, plantains, and tropical shrubs, wherever it has not been reclaimed to make one of the exquisitely tidy settlements, with their trim bungalows and flawless roads and plots of grass, where the Canal Zone employees live.

The canal itself has three characters—first, the splendid locks, which are not only a monument of engineering skill, but are built with a simple and massive dignity; secondly, the broad expanse of the Gatun Lake, where the dammed-up waters of the Chagres River have made an inland sea, still broken in parts by the summits of the tropical forest which it has submerged; and, thirdly, the long, narrow cut through the central range which divides the Gatun Lake from the locks on the Pacific side. The *Renown* looked enormous in the narrow parts of the canal—as much too large for her surroundings as if she had been steaming past the University barges on the Isis at Oxford.

The voyage through the Pacific was made throughout in holiday vein. After a very pleasant stay of twenty-four hours at San Diego, the *Renown* anchored off Honolulu on April 13. The official ceremonies on shore were brief, and the greater part of the day was given up to a Hawaiian pageant, a Hawaiian feast at night, and to the great Hawaiian recreation of surf-riding on Waikiki Beach. One of the charming customs of the islanders is to cover the visitor with wreaths, and the Prince accumulated a very large number of these. Legend says that if these wreaths are thrown overboard by the departing guest in time for the tide to carry them ashore, his return at some time to Honolulu is absolutely assured.

Between Honolulu and Fiji the *Renown* crossed the line, with all the ancient naval ceremonies by which that proceeding is always celebrated in His Majesty's ships. So much has been written of the excellent fooling of King Neptune and his Court that there is no need to describe it further here.

At Fiji the main novelty was a great reception and war dance by the assembled Fijian tribes. The Fijian is a splendid specimen of the Polynesian islander, a type which displays strong racial similarity from Hawaii to

New Zealand, where the Maoris are the southernmost representatives of their kind. The peculiarity of the Fijian is a magnificent head of fuzzy hair, which he prefers to the various forms of picturesque head-dress worn by other islanders. The Fijian photographs are easily distinguished by this trait.

The most important period of the tour, the visits to New Zealand and then Australia, followed immediately upon Fiji. In rather uncertain weather the *Renown* plunged southwards out of the tropics, and anchored in Auckland Harbour, under an exquisite blue sky, early on April 24.

In its main outlines the tour through the two great Southern Dominions resembled, so far as the leading arrangements were concerned, the tour through Canada. As in the older Dominion, the Prince was greeted everywhere by enthusiastic masses of returned soldiers, by splendid gatherings of school-children, and enormous cheering crowds wherever he drove. He also held great popular receptions in all the cities in which he stayed. In Melbourne and Sydney, the two largest cities visited in the tour, it was computed that more than fifty thousand people filed close past him during the hours given to this ceremony ; and even so there were still thousands waiting outside. The gatherings of school-children were even more massive than in Canada, so many as from ten to twenty thousand children being often gathered on large spaces, such as cricket grounds, where they formed themselves into designs and mottoes with the prettiest possible effect and with wonderful discipline. Another very charming feature of these displays was the Maypole Dances, which were often carried out by hundreds of tiny girls dancing in small groups, each round its maypole, the ribbons matching the children's frocks.

THE AUSTRALASIAN TOUR

Both Australia and New Zealand provided one element quite different from Canada. Both peoples are devoted to horses, to stock, and to all forms of sport. The Prince attended large numbers of race meetings in both Dominions, and was always greeted by vast crowds. Usually he rode out on the course during the afternoon and started a race himself. He also attended a number of very fine agricultural shows.

The greater part of the tour through New Zealand was done by rail. The Prince left Auckland on April 27 for Rotorua, where he inspected all the sights of that volcanic wonderland, and also attended a magnificent Maori display. It was delightful to observe the combination in the Maori people of ancient customs and modern tastes. Many a Maori lady, clad in the ancient finery of her race and rolling her eyes with the frenzy of a savage, danced up towards the Prince, produced a Kodak from nowhere, snapshotted the Prince's group with practised skill, and danced away again once more in the ancient Maori style.

Almost all the settled parts of the North Island were visited by train, and on May 5 the Prince made his entry into the capital of the Dominion, Wellington. The scenes which awaited him there will not easily be forgotten by those who took part in them. From Wellington the *Renown* bore him across Cook's Strait to Picton, in the north of the South Island. From that point he travelled by motor and train across the mountains to the mining districts on the west coast, and then through the magnificent Otira Gorge in the Alpine range down upon Christchurch and the wonderful Canterbury Plains, which lie in miles of rolling land between the snow-clad Alps and the blue Pacific main.

After Christchurch, Dunedin. Here the population is largely Scottish in origin, and after the tropics the rigours of Otago were severe ; but neither at Dunedin nor at Invercargill, still further south, did climate cool the enthusiasm of the crowds which greeted the Prince everywhere. He was back in Christchurch on May 21, and sailed from Lyttelton, the port of Christchurch, at dawn next day.

Owing to the great distances, the tour round Australia was carried out in much larger part by sea. The *Renown* cast anchor off Melbourne Heads at dawn on May 26. It was impossible for her to enter the heads till the fog bank lifted, and the Prince therefore made his entry in a destroyer appropriately named the *Anzac*. So tense and so universal was the enthusiasm roused by his presence there, that on the completion of his Victorian programme, which lasted about ten days, he had to take a week's holiday in order to enjoy a few days' rest and normal life. On June 13 he left Melbourne in the *Renown* for New South Wales, halting for a night to inspect the Australian Naval College at Jervis Bay, and making his entry into Sydney Harbour on the morning of June 16th. As the great ship, escorted by the Australian fleet, came through the Heads and slowly rounded the famous turn in the harbour which opens up the endless bays and reaches of that magnificent anchorage, hundreds of yachts and boats and ferries came out to meet and greet their guest. Sydney's passion for its harbour is proverbial, even in Sydney itself. " How do you like our harbour ? " shouted many voices to the *Renown*—answered, very fittingly, by " How do you like our ship ? "

In Sydney the scenes which had made the Melbourne visit memorable were repeated every day ; and, as in

THE AUSTRALASIAN TOUR

Melbourne, the Prince spent three or four days outside the capital visiting by train some of the more important districts of the State. On June 25th he embarked once more in the *Renown*, which laid her course south and west across the Great Australian Bight for Western Australia—a voyage equivalent to that from Portsmouth to the Atlantic coast of Canada. The Bight was at its worst; great seas, driven by a south-west gale right across the Indian Ocean from the Cape of Good Hope, broke in mighty masses of green water and flying foam on the fo'csle of the huge ship as she ploughed her way steadily to the west. In spite of all she anchored off Albany, as always, punctually to time.

The greater part of the Western Australian visit was spent in Perth, the capital, with visits to Fremantle, the port of Perth, and to the more important districts in the neighbourhood. On July 8th the Prince left Perth for the great gold cities at Kalgoorlie and Boulder, and then entrained in the Trans-Australian Line for Adelaide, the capital of South Australia.

The railway journey was made in great comfort across the treeless waste which divides Kalgoorlie and Port Augusta, the eastern terminus of the line, and the Prince paid a sincere tribute to the organisation of this great Commonwealth railway, which has been in operation only since the third year of the war. Half-way across the plain he witnessed a Corroboree by Australian blacks, a dying race, now very few in numbers, which were not encountered at any other point in the tour.

Adelaide is a charming city, most beautifully laid out with open spaces and parks. After a delightful stay of four days, the Prince was once more on board the *Renown* on July 16th, heading for Hobart, the capital of Tasmania where, in addition to the two days' visit to the capital itself, he made a journey by rail across the island to the largest city in the northern area, Launceston. He sailed from Hobart again on July 23rd, landed in Sydney on July 25th, and went straight up to Queensland from there by rail for the last State visit of the Australian tour.

Brisbane, the capital of Queensland, received him with a fervour which seemed to have gathered force from the libellous assumption made in some public prints that Queensland, with its very strong Labour Government, would be less anxious to receive him than other Australian States. Nowhere was he more ecstatically welcomed or delightfully entertained. As he left the frontier at Wallangarra again on August 5th, he stepped from the Queensland to the New South Wales train across a pathway of wattle blossom and under a beautiful arch of the same flower. The yellow gold of the wattle, trembling in the brilliant sunshine of that sunny land, bespoke the radiant pleasure with which Australia had received him from end to end.

The next week was spent almost entirely in the saddle, seeing something of the varied activities of up-country life. The Prince rounded up mobs of cattle, cut out bullocks from other mobs as station policy required, inspected the great shearing sheds and sheared a sheep himself, and raced in the improvised races which are one of the features of every little settlement in the Australian bush. On August 14th he was back again in Sydney to take his final farewell of the Governor-General, Sir Ronald Munro-Ferguson; the Prime Minister of the Commonwealth, Mr. Hughes; and other representatives of the Australian Governments. It looked as if he would have to leave Australia on August 19th without his English mail, but the Australian Air Force brought his mail-bags across the Australian continent from west to east with wonderful resource, and put them on board the *Renown* inside Sydney Heads on the evening of the 19th, just before she turned her head north-east for Fiji.

The short return visit to Fiji was followed by an equally short, but most interesting, visit to Apia, the capital of British Samoa, once the home of Robert Louis Stevenson. Here the native Samoan tribes, headed by their ancient chiefs, received the Prince with the most picturesque of Samoan dances and native displays. The Prince had afterwards just time to drive up to Vailima, the old house which Stevenson built for himself three miles above Apia town. For many years it had been the headquarters of the German Governor, and Stevenson's own favourite fireplace was surmounted by a copy of Lenbach's portrait of Bismarck, while the adjoining room was adorned with an oil painting of guard-mounting at Potsdam. Now Stevenson's home is the headquarters of the Administrator appointed by New Zealand under the mandate which has placed the Island in British hands. The Prince climbed up the hill above the house to Stevenson's lofty tomb, which stands upon a densely wooded shoulder overlooking Vailima steeply on one side and the distant bay and coral reef of Apia on the other, which, on that afternoon, framed the massive lines of the *Renown*.

After Samoa, Honolulu, Acapulco—a most picturesque port in Mexico—the Panama Canal once more, and then the British West Indies again at Trinidad. From Trinidad the Prince went southward in H.M.S. *Calcutta* to visit British Guiana, the only British Colony in the South American Continent. He returned to the *Renown* once more in Trinidad, where his stay was most enjoyable, and visited in quick succession the Windward Islands, with their capital at Grenada, an exquisite old-world port, the Leeward Islands, with their capital at Antigua, and close to it the old haven of English Harbour, where Nelson refitted for his last voyage home, hardly changed by a stone since Nelson's time.

Jamaica had, unfortunately, to be omitted, owing to a serious epidemic. The last visit of the tour was to Bermuda, where the Prince's arrival coincided with the celebrations of the tercentenary of the Bermudan Legislature, the oldest Colonial legislature in the Empire to-day. The *Renown* sailed from Bermuda on October 4th, and secured alongside the jetty at Portsmouth once more in the early hours of October 11th.

During the cruise in the West Indies, a sad tragedy occurred among the menagerie in the *Renown*. The Prince of Wales's wallaby, given to him in May by an Australian girl in the country near Melbourne, had become the greatest of all the many pets on board. Less than two feet high, in form like a wee kangaroo, he was entirely fearless and always full of life. He had become the soul of the after-cabin during the homeward voyage ; and surely no one who looks at his photograph here can fail to realise how insinuating was his charm. He came ashore for exercise at Trinidad, and in a tragic moment ate some poisonous plant or flower in the grounds of Government House. Brandy, castor oil, and the most devoted care were all of no avail—" Digger " died that evening, mourned most bitterly by the Prince and all his Staff. He is buried in the Government House garden at Trinidad, and none of his friends will ever pass that way without a pilgrimage to his tiny memorial stone.

Little " Digger " took his name from the Australian and New Zealand troops, who made that title famous in the war and ultimately bestowed it upon the Prince himself. With all its ties of common service and experience, it seems in retrospect to stand for even more than the soldiers meant who called it after the Prince's motor in the streets. Comradeship, as the Prince has said, is the key to all well-being and happiness in the democratic life of the Empire to-day—comradeship between British nation and nation, comradeship between all walks of life within each nation's ranks. Never surely in any Empire was such mutual love and loyalty between Prince and People as shines from the pictures in this book. First moulded in the comradeship of war, that mutual tie between the King's lieges and the King has been broadened by the Prince's travels into a world-wide and enduring comradeship of peace.

The
Australasian
Tour

AUSTRALIA

THE PRINCE AND "DIGGER"

PORTSMOUTH

PORTSMOUTH, MARCH 16th, 1920.

THE CAPTAIN   THE ADMIRAL   THE PRINCE

H.M.S. RENOWN

DIVINE SERVICE ON BOARD

BARBADOS

WELCOME TO
BARBADOS

INSPECTING THE
GUARD OF HONOUR
BRIDGETOWN,
BARBADOS

THE BOYS' GUARD OF HONOUR.

PANAMA

H.M.S. RENOWN
IN THE
CULEBRA CUT

TALKING TO
THE BRITISH
WEST INDIAN
SERGEANT

IN GATUN LAKE, PANAMA

SAN DIEGO

IN THE
STADIUM

SPEAKING
THROUGH THE
MAGNAVOX
HORNS.

WITH THE
GOVERNOR OF
CALIFORNIA

CALIFORNIA

IN THE
BARGE,
GOING ASHORE
AT
SAN DIEGO

WITH BILL NYE,
OF THE
STATE
DEPARTMENT

ON SAN DIEGO GOLF COURSE.

HONOLULU

PRESENTATION
OF
HAWAIIAN
WREATHS

WEARING
THE WREATHS

GREETS A RETURNED SOLDIER

CROSSING THE LINE

WATCHING
THE FUN

ADDRESSING KING NEPTUNE AFTER RECEIVING
THE ORDER OF THE EQUATORIAL BATH

CROSSING THE LINE

LATHERED
WITH ALL KINDS

OF STUFF—
AND SHAVED

BEFORE THE BATH

FIJI

NATIVES WAITING FOR THE PRINCE

PRESENTATION OF MATS

THE INSPECTION

H.M.S. "RENOWN"

WITH HIS ORDERLY OUTSIDE THE SQUASH RACQUET COURT

NEW ZEALAND

ESCORTED
UP THE BAY
AT
AUCKLAND

ARRIVAL IN NEW ZEALAND

CHILDREN'S DEMONSTRATION, AUCKLAND

NEW ZEALAND

WITH SIR JOHN WARD, EX-PREMIER OF NEW ZEALAND

THE CLERKS OF THE COURSE AT AUCKLAND RACES

NEW ZEALAND

WATCHING NATIVE CEREMONIES AT ROTORUA. H.R.H. AND DR. POMARE

A MAORI TRIBE

NEW ZEALAND

MAORI GIRLS

MAORI WARRIORS

J

NEW ZEALAND

AMONG THE GEYSERS OF ROTORUA

WITH THE MAORIS

NEW ZEALAND

AT GOVERNMENT HOUSE,
WELLINGTON

WITH THE PREMIER,
MR. MASSEY

CHILDREN GREET THE PRINCE WITH
PAMPAS GRASS AT NEW PLYMOUTH

NEW ZEALAND

HURRAH!
FOR THE
PRINCE

WOLF CUBS

BRIDGE BUILT BY BOY SCOUTS.

NEW ZEALAND

THE TRAVELLING GUARD IN NEW ZEALAND

THE PRINCE SURPRISES A PICNIC PARTY

NEW ZEALAND

ON THE WAY TO THE RACES, CHRISTCHURCH

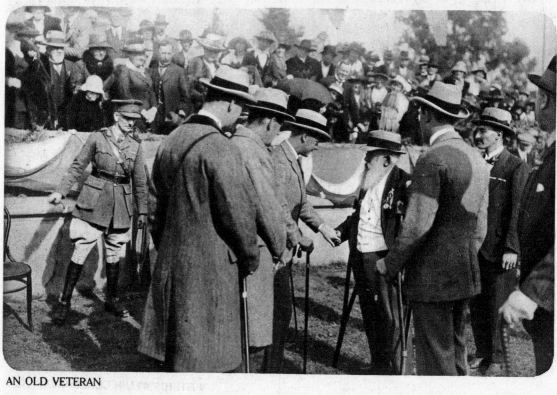

AN OLD VETERAN

AUSTRALIA

WITH HIS WELSH GUARD ORDERLIES

AUSTRALIA

ON BOARD H.M.A.S. "ANZAC"

WITH MR. HUGHES, VIEWING THE FLEET AT MELBOURNE

H.M.A.S. "AUSTRALIA" ASTERN OF "RENOWN"

RETURNING THE SALUTE OF
H.M.A.S. "AUSTRALIA"

AUSTRALIA

ON BOARD
H.M.A.S. "ANZAC"

"RENOWN" CHEERING THE
PRINCE DURING
THE REVIEW

H.R.H.
ADDRESSES
THE MEN

AUSTRALIA

JUTLAND DAY, MELBOURNE

A PRESENTATION OF FLOWERS

AUSTRALIA

UNDER CAMERA FIRE

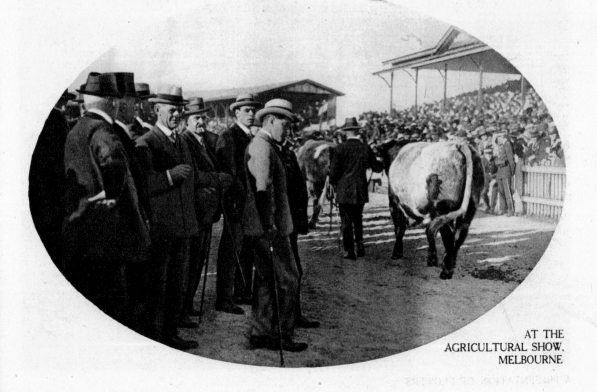

AT THE
AGRICULTURAL SHOW,
MELBOURNE

AUSTRALIA

TREE PLANTING

SHAKING HANDS
WITH THE
SCHOOLGIRLS

THE MAYPOLE

AUSTRALIA

H.R.H. AND MR. HUGHES READY FOR THE GOLD MINE, BENDIGO

AUSTRALIA

FOOTBALL MATCH AT THE ROYAL AUSTRALIAN NAVAL COLLEGE, JERVIS BAY

GREETING MR. HUGHES ON ARRIVAL AT SYDNEY

AUSTRALIA

INSPECTING CADETS AT MILITARY COLLEGE, DUNTROON

GUARD OF HONOUR AT SYDNEY

SHIPS ILLUMINATED IN SYDNEY HARBOUR

AUSTRALIA

MANY HAPPY RETURNS, SYDNEY, JUNE 23rd, 1920

AUSTRALIA

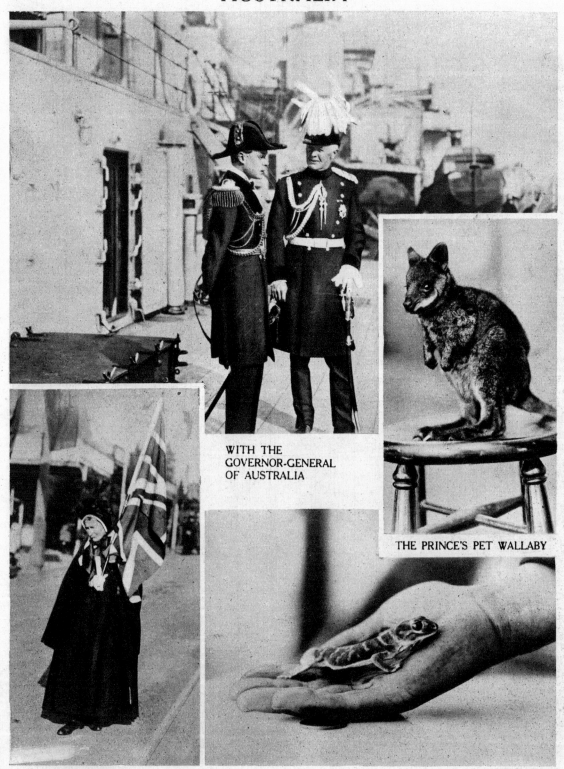

WITH THE
GOVERNOR-GENERAL
OF AUSTRALIA

THE PRINCE'S PET WALLABY

"THE LADY WITH THE
FLAG" OF HOBART

PET LIZARD

K

AUSTRALIA

AT THE NEW CAPITAL CITY, CANBERRA

AT MILITARY COLLEGE, DUNTROON

AUSTRALIA

ARRIVAL
AT PERTH

INSPECTION
AT FREMANTLE

CHATTING TO CAPT. WATSON, FIRST RECIPIENT IN WESTERN AUSTRALIA OF ROYAL
HUMANE SOCIETY'S MEDAL

AUSTRALIA

THE RAILWAY ACCIDENT

AUSTRALIA

TRIES HIS HAND WITH A SAW

WOOD CHOPPING

AUSTRALIA

UNVEILING STATUE TO KING EDWARD AT ADELAIDE

IN DOCTOR'S ROBES, ADELAIDE UNIVERSITY

AUSTRALIA

ARRIVAL IN BRISBANE

AT THE CATTLE SHOW, BRISBANE

AUSTRALIA

ON ASCOT RACECOURSE, BRISBANE

POSING FOR PHOTOGRAPH
ON BOARD H.M.S. "RENOWN"

AUSTRALIAN NATIVE BEAR
PRESENTED TO THE PRINCE

AUSTRALIA

IN THE
BACK BLOCKS

AT A SHEEP-DOG TRIAL

K*

AUSTRALIA

RANDWICK RACECOURSE, SYDNEY

THE PADDOCK AT RANDWICK

AUSTRALIA

A MORNING
GALLOP.

OVER THE STICKS

AUSTRALIA

ON THE WAY TO THE BACK BLOCKS

HAS HIS PHOTOGRAPH TAKEN BY A LAME GIRL AT A COUNTRY RACE MEETING

A CLOSE FINISH. RANDWICK RACECOURSE

SAMOA

NATIVE WAR CANOE ESCORTING
THE PRINCE INTO APIA

AN
INTERESTED
SPECTATOR

SAMOAN CHIEFS

SAMOA

WATCHING THE DANCES

GREETING A NATIVE CHIEF

MEXICO

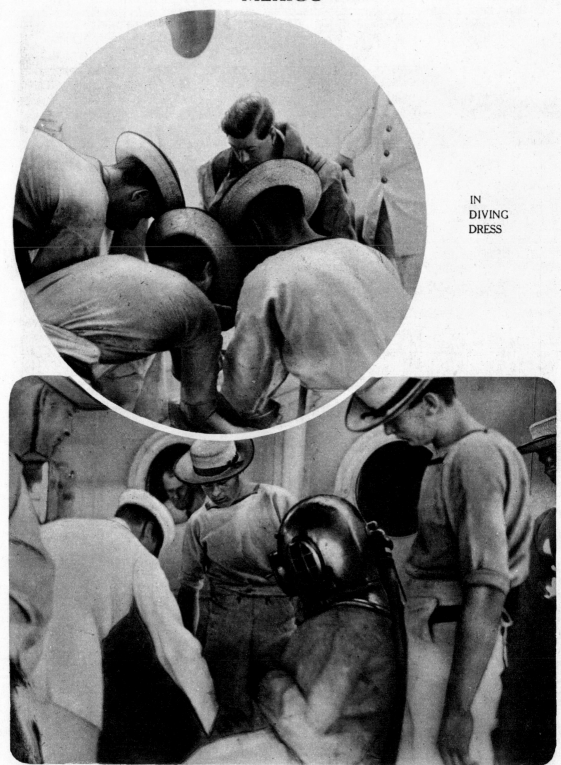

IN
DIVING
DRESS

WEST INDIES

ON THE BEACH AT GRENADA

AT PORT-OF-SPAIN, TRINIDAD

BRITISH GUIANA & BERMUDA

STARTING THE RACE FOR THE PRINCE OF WALES CUP, GEORGETOWN

ST. GEORGES, BERMUDA

PORTSMOUTH

PORTSMOUTH, OCTOBER 11th, 1920

WALKING TO INSPECT THE GUARD OF HONOUR

ROYAL TRAIN LEAVES FOR LONDON

LONDON

WELCOME HOME